PEWSEY RAMBLES

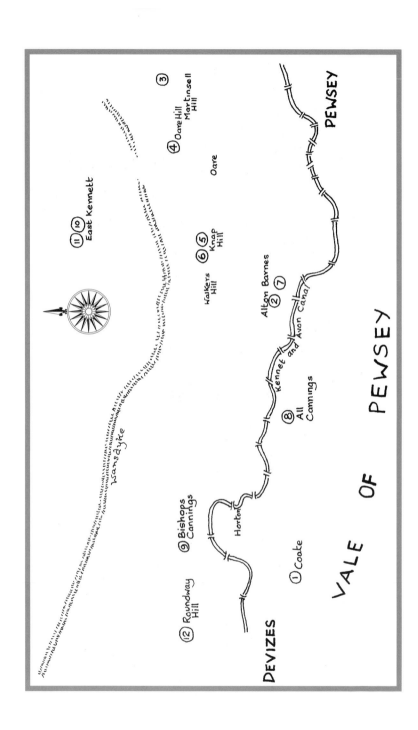

PEWSEY RAMBLES

Walks on the Pewsey Downs and surrounding area

James Alsop

Ex Libris Press

Published in 2008 by
EX LIBRIS PRESS
16A St John's Road
St Helier
Jersey   JE2 3LD

Origination by Ex Libris Press

Printed by Cromwell Press
Trowbridge, Wiltshire

ISBN 978-1-903341-03-0

The engraving on page 30 is from an old edition of
Chambers Encyclopaedia; those on pages 38, 42, 48,
57 and 74 are by Thomas Bewick, 1753-1795

*To Jamie Campbell, a friend as close as a brother, who,
though geographically distant, is always close in spirit.*

CONTENTS

THE WALKS

Introducing the Pewsey Downs

In a county already dominated by downland and liberally sprinkled with scenic delights, the Pewsey Downs reign supreme. Further, there are multiple reasons why this is so. The downs occupy the highest ground in the county, topping out at 295 metres (according to OS Explorer maps) or just under 1000 feet above sea level, thus everywhere else in Wiltshire is beneath them, by a few metres at least. Unsurprisingly therefore they offer remarkable views, often to every point of the compass, enticing walkers, photographers and other lovers of these downs, to turn full circle time and time again, in order to comprehend the true splendour of their surroundings. However, superior height is just the tip of the iceberg! The steep, south facing, individualistic slopes that often fall in unbroken lines to the valley floor, dominate the Vale of Pewsey, over which they proudly stand, as if to guard the vale from danger. In addition, the short cropped, soft and springy terrain is almost perfect for walking, providing the delightful combination of firm but gentle underfoot conditions, enabling the miles to slip by effortlessly.

Another attractive feature of the Pewsey Downs is the climate (see pages 20-21 for more details), for it is here that an exciting juxtaposition can be enjoyed, between lowland and upland conditions. The former ensures moderate rainfall, lots of sunshine and the rarity of severe conditions, such that make them an enjoyable alternative when experienced; the latter providing an upland flavour when strong winds howl over the downland plateau and exposed summits, especially if accompanied by wintry showers.

Neither should it pass unnoticed that a significant area of these downs form a nature reserve where sometimes rare wild flowers, butterflies, birds and other wildlife can be viewed and studied. Further, the protection such a special area enjoys ensures that the scope for inappropriate development is at least curtailed and access for walkers and nature lovers enhanced. Fortuitously, the downs also fall within the south-western corner of the North Wessex Downs Area of Outstanding Natural Beauty (AONB) which although regionally administered, by district and county councils, has objectives similar to that of national parks. Their main purpose – conserving and enhancing natural beauty – though not as extensive and all-encompassing as that of national parks, ensures that stringent planning policies and development control are, by statute, a top priority. The peace of mind such protection provides, when passing over a much loved landscape, is a real blessing, especially when considering the current pressure on planners to surrender land for huge house building projects, with apparent disregard for the impact on precious countryside, and the recreational benefits that so many of us enjoy, both on a sedentary and active basis.

The Pewsey Downs possess many more qualities beyond the scope of this guidebook, but one remaining feature I wish to comment on is the rich variety of colour seen on and from them. The well known expression, 'every shade of green' takes on new meaning when traversing these hills, especially on bright, clear days. But the passing seasons ensure green, though dominant, is far from the only colour to preoccupy the wanderer. Autumn's golden hues, winter's deep blue skies (when settled conditions prevail) spring's burst of almost incomprehensible new life and colourful diversity, summer's chessboard patchwork dominated by shades of brown, all contribute to a riot of year round colour, for which the downs are justly famed.

Here then dear reader is an area of immense appeal, where crowds, congestion and the worries of everyday life can be left behind, and peace, serenity, exhilaration and excitement enjoyed in abundance.

Defining the scope of the downs

Surveying the downs from the Vale of Pewsey at their feet, might convey the impression that they are easily definable. However, appearances and first impressions can be deceiving. Furthermore, historical associations can also complicate matters, as years of tradition have a powerful influence over the perceived scope of named landscapes.

There are, perhaps, a number of reasons why the scope of these downs, in particular, is not straightforward to establish. First, the Pewsey Downs Nature Reserve (covering Knap Hill to Milk Hill) is a very small area, but boasts the only reference to them, featured on OS maps (Landranger and Explorer) by name.

Second, the downs are part of two larger areas, which therefore produces a kind of layering system of sorts. They sit at the southern end of the Marlborough Downs, which cover a far larger region, while the latter are themselves part of the North Wessex Downs AONB, a substantially larger area again.

Third, the Vale of Pewsey might well be said to mirror the downs and yes, they do gradually loose their steep southern profile (specifically, on Easton Hill), just to the north of Horton, one of three villages which herald the western terminus of the vale (the other two being Coate further south and Bishops Cannings to the north-west). However, when the downs are viewed from Etchilhampton Hill, they appear to continue seamlessly to Roundway, some three and a half miles further west.

Deciding where the northern boundary lies is also not without dispute, the gentler northern slopes of the downs themselves being one possibility, or perhaps the Wansdyke – a man-made but nevertheless ancient feature – another. Both are somewhat arbitrary boundaries, though for different reasons: the former, because the downs flow northwards without interruption, the latter, because of its man-made origins. Browsing the detailed works of Wiltshire's leading authorities on such matters (John Chandler, author of *The Vale of Pewsey*, and Ken Watts, author of *The Marlborough Downs* – see Further Reading, page 76), by inference and implication it appears that the Pewsey and Marlborough Downs overlap, but beyond the Wansdyke (between Knapp Hill and Tan Hill especially) one steps into the undisputed region of the Marlborough Downs.

To the east, perhaps the least ambiguous boundary is to be found, for Martinsell Hill sits majestically above Eastern Wiltshire, whose steep, tumbling slopes face east as well as south, and are completely cut off from other downland regions, visible to the south-east and north-east.

If such attempts to clarify the scope of the downs appear

ambiguous, don't concern yourself too much, for there is a definite silver lining. The very ambiguity discussed enables a degree of discretion to be used, thus the scope for walks in this guidebook has been deliberately extended beyond the region perhaps conceptualised by most as the Pewsey Downs. This though is not just blatant expediency, but contains an obvious logic already alluded to. Should you be sceptical, why not ascend Etchilhampton Hill and pour over the scene at leisure, and see the seamless stretch of downland before your eyes. Not only may you be lost for words as you attempt to comprehend their drama and beauty, but you will also witness the extent and homogeneity of the downs hereabouts.

Downland geology and history in brief

The geological character of the Pewsey Downs is central to their smooth, steep and pleasing appeal. Beneath a very thin layer of topsoil, chalk dominates! Chalk is relatively soft and thus the downland here and elsewhere has eroded quite easily, resulting in the smoothness of form and outline so attractive to the eye. Further, being especially porous, streams are not found on these downs, water collecting in the Pewsey Vale instead, after passing rapidly through the chalk.

Some may argue that one consequence of such geological features is a tendency to uniform landscapes, however, a brief visit to this delightful region (on foot of course) will dispel all thoughts of monotony, quite probably instead, sending a surge of enthusiasm through your veins, urging you to stride up onto the various hills and plateaux, consumed with anticipation at the thrills to be enjoyed, as you study their unique character.

This landscape is also one of genuine historical significance. Ancient burial grounds, ridgeways and other artefacts are much in evidence, even for those who care to pay no more than a passing glance; and perhaps most significantly of all, the Wansdyke passes through the heart of the area from east to west. This dyke, thought probably to have been constructed as early as the fifth or sixth century, by Britons to deter Saxon invaders, is little short of extraordinary. Commencing at Inkpen in the east and extending all the way to the Bristol Channel in the west (some fifty miles), the thrill of standing and striding out upon it, with so much history beneath one's feet, and such gorgeous views all around, is almost indescribable. Moreover, nowhere is it in finer condition nor better placed as a hilltop belvedere, than between Milk Hill and Morgan's Hill. It will come as no surprise therefore, that several of the walks (six to be precise) at some point or another, include at least a small stretch along it.

Downland summits

I pondered long and hard before deciding to include this brief description of the prominent summits visited, if following the routes included in this book. The reason being that lists have a notorious reputation for attracting list tickers and portfolio builders, which though understandable in some regions of the UK, is inappropriate on these downs. Put another way, my fear is, that a list of summits could result in a small number of zealots dashing up and down them, causing unnecessary erosion and missing the best of the downs, which are to be enjoyed via long and detailed exploration, on the summits, along the steep scarp edge, in the vale and even from the Kennet and Avon Canal.

However, convinced eventually that it is unlikely that such a trend might occur (owing to the modest altitude of these hills and the limited distances and effort required to ascend them), I decided that it would be a pity not to at least mention, in a systematic manner, the unique views experienced from each, or the character and shape of the hills themselves. Thus what follows is an east to west appraisal of the key summits, followed by additional comments on the three delightful outliers (this time west to east) namely Etchilhampton Hill, Woodborough Hill and Picked Hill, the latter of which is not included in the walks due to access problems, but receives a justly deserved mention.

▲ Martinsell Hill (289m)
Second only in height to Milk Hill and Tan Hill, and superior in every other way, Martinsell serves as a thrilling highlight to many a

downland expedition. Rising abruptly above Eastern Wiltshire and Berkshire (the latter some ten miles distant), Martinsell's summit offers mesmerising views; and where the ridge turns west towards Giant's Grave, the Vale of Pewsey comes into view from end-to-end when clear conditions prevail. The relative ease of ascent and spectacular vistas awaiting those who climb it, make this (in my view) one of the finest viewpoints of inland, south-west England. Further, the clean, smooth and steep profile of the downs hereabouts creates a sense of drama, more common in upland regions of the UK.

▲ Giant's Grave (250m)

Nowhere else on these downs, or in Wiltshire for that matter, does a hill exhibit 'mountain in miniature' credentials more effectively. Viewed from the lane leading east from the village of Oare, this hill rises in one clean sweep of improbable steepness, with sharply defined slopes falling evenly on both sides to the valley floor. The brief but exhilarating climb to its summit terminates in a remarkable view, capable of riveting the gaze of the most jaded walker! It is vital, therefore, to ensure that any planned walk involving a visit to this summit is enjoyed on a clear day, enabling the fullest appreciation of the scenic delights, demanding your attention this way and that.

▲ Huish Hill (261m)

Despite the lack of any definable summit, this hill stands proudly above the village of Oare, and an ascent from there represents a steep and thrilling climb. Near the top a bench provides the opportunity to rest and admire the view from yet another unique angle. Giant's Grave is prominent; so too the horseshoe shaped hillsides arcing round to the north and to Oare Hill.

▲ Golden Ball Hill (268m)

The name appears to apply to a substantial area of downland rather than a distinct summit, but without doubt its charms are unmistake-able, not least because of the long spur it throws down to the valley floor, which invites the explorer and breaks any tendency to mono-tony in the downland scene. Here too, one can stride out high on the downs, right beside their steep southern scarp edge, gazing over the

Steep, majestic and compelling. For profile, individuality and far-reaching views, Martinsell Hill is perhaps the fairest of the fair

Giant's Grave – a mountain in miniature from this angle

Tan Hill from Clifford's Hill

Woodborough Hill, viewed from the canal bridge, in the tiny settlement of Honeystreet

vale simultaneously.

▲ Knap Hill (261m)

From the car park besides the adjacent road over the downs, it is an easy ascent to the summit of this lovely hill. However, not until the very last moment is the remarkable view revealed. The first time I beheld it, it took my breath away (and still does) as, from its pretty perch, the downs' eastern aspect can be viewed to great advantage; so too the Vale of Pewsey.

Often featuring at the start of a walk, this hill serves as the perfect enticement to stroll out along the downs, anticipating and enjoying beautiful vistas with almost every step.

▲ Walker's Hill (262m)

There could scarcely be a more appropriate name for this exposed summit from which almost the entire width of Wiltshire can be horizontally appraised. An ancient hilltop burial ground (Adam's Grave) conveniently provides an aesthetically pleasing viewing gallery, and gives the impression of a ridge top experience simultaneously. Further, this hill's long southern slopes fall gracefully almost all the way to the village of Alton Barnes in the vale below.

To the east Ham Hill, the forerunner to Inkpen Beacon, can be clearly identified some fifteen miles distant on the Berkshire border, while away in the south-west the Deverills can be spotted lifting their lofty summits above the surrounding land. And to the west the Vale of Pewsey seems never ending; in fact locals have laid claim to spotting Dundry Hill (south of Bristol) and even the Mendip Mast on exceptionally clear days! Neither should one forget the superb opportunity this hill provides to admire the downs themselves, due in no small part to its position, some way south of the surrounding downland summits.

▲ Milk Hill (295m)

There is more than a touch of irony about the summit of this hill. Despite being the highest point in Wiltshire, it is scarcely a summit at all, but rather just an extended plateau, with few obvious features of merit. In addition, it is also an enclosed, cultivated area (which is unusual for the Pewsey Downs), offering neither open access nor rights of way in the immediate vicinity. However there is no need to be disappointed, for it is where the slopes of the hill begin to tumble steeply to the west that true drama is to be found. Here too access is assured, the ground uncultivated and the altitude just a few metres lower than the featureless highest point.

▲ Tan Hill (294m)

Tan Hill shares many characteristics with its near neighbour, topping out just one metre lower and crowning a downland plateau. The trig point also sits within an enclosed area, although open access arrangements and a right of way running north to south enable one to pause within a few metres of it, just to the east of a fence. Further, all around the views are magnificent and, just a short distance from the summit, uncultivated land provides a true hilltop environment.

Both this hill and its slightly higher neighbour provide a salutory lesson for any summit list tickers, this being that the highest points in a given range are not by definition superior to all others.

▲ Clifford's Hill (243m)

This is a hill walker's dream! When accessed from the south, after a dramatic but brief and straightforward ascent, the summit of this hill provides a breathtaking view in every direction. Views south over the Vale of Pewsey (Etchilhampton Hill being particularly prominent) are delightful, while to the west Roundway Hill, Morgan's Hill and the far western end of the downs themselves complete a scene of downland perfection. If more encouragement were needed, the small, twin summit area provides a special hilltop ambience and solitude, to which you may find yourself drawn many times over.

▲ Morgan's Hill (260m)

Though this hill may be well beyond the accepted boundaries of the Pewsey Downs, it is linked in more ways than one. First, the Wansdyke provides an umbilical cord between Tan Hill and its own lofty summit; second, the path between them (along the dyke) never falls below 175m; third, the environs of the hill also form a significant nature reserve and fourth, the hill falls quite steeply to the vale beneath. However, on this occasion the most dramatic views and steepest slopes fall to the north, affording views beyond Calne to Chippenham and out over the north of the county. Note also, that for the finest panorama, one needs to descend slightly into the uncultivated nature reserve where a bench provides an additional enticement to pause, and enjoy an unhurried study of the exquisite Wiltshire scenery laid out before you.

▲ Roundway Hill (242m)

The most west facing of any featured in this guide book, Roundway Hill is proudly a member of the club of those whose highest point is not the most exciting. Such an obvious observation is robustly supported by the remarkable terminus of the hill where slopes fall steeply westwards to gentle countryside below. However, steepness is not the only virtue of Roundway's western face, for here the downs exhibit finger like spurs which encourage detailed study and exploration. This is also the location of yet another nature reserve, affording protection for rare birds and plant life and providing a delightful environment for outdoor walking enthusiasts and more casual strollers.

▲ Etchilhampton Hill (190m)

The best vantage point from which to admire this hill's aesthetic merits is the downs themselves, there being no better viewpoint than the summit of Clifford's Hill. From here, the hill's appeal is obvious. By contrast, when commencing an ascent via the lane from Coate, it appears, temporarily, that no hill is there to be climbed. But when the road is forsaken and the north-eastern spur encountered, superb views of the downs compensate many times over for any sense of anti-climax. Then from the summit, a unique view of the downs and all western outliers – Morgan's Hill and Roundway Hill especially – provides a wonderful opportunity to absorb the synergy that links Roundway Hill in the west to Giant's Grave in the east. In brief, the gentle ascent and sumptuous views ensure that no visit to this hill will be in vain.

▲ Woodborough Hill (205m)

Describing the charms of this hill is no easy task, thus you had better ascend it to appreciate its myriad qualities for yourself. Viewed from the downs it is striking as much for its pretty appearance as any other virtues. What's more, approaching from the south, via the Kennet and Avon Canal, the ease of ascent fails to give the slightest indication of the drama soon to unfold! Suddenly, and at the very last moment, as the summit is reached, an unforgettable panorama bursts into view. For those wishing to enjoy a grandstand view of Wiltshire's finest downland, this is the place to be! The view ahead and to the left (west) and right (east) is completely dominated by the profile of the downs' steep, southern scarp edge, while the small summit plateau itself, provides one with a remarkably lofty sensation, as if suspended some distance above the Vale of Pewsey.

▲ Picked Hill (202m)

Tiny but bold, conical, symmetrical, aesthetically pleasing, conspicuous and arresting, this hill is a mountain in all but stature, especially when approached from the south. However, it is more than a little ironic that in an area so blessed with excellent access, this hill is beyond the legal bounds of the most careful of walkers. Further, despite consisting of uncultivated ground, which in fact extends all the way to the canal towpath, and other obvious, potential links, no right of way, open access or Department for the Environment and Rural Affairs (DEFRA) arrangement exists, thus it remains tantalisingly forbidden. It is hoped that in the not-too-distant future formal access will be permitted, but sadly for now at least, we must be content just to look and admire but not to climb.

One final thought! Is it not extraordinary that an extensive area of downland such as this should possess so many distinctive and attractive hilltops? Downland, though almost always attractive in my view, is more typically known for long, almost unbroken hillsides that while elevated, consist of little to distinguish one area from another. But here, on the Pewsey Downs, many of the summits listed are hills of unique character, rewarding repeated visits, with their stunning vantage points and personal welcome.

Enjoy the summits, but walk all the bits in between too.

The Kennet & Avon Canal

Despite the fact that this guidebook focuses on the extensive downland and outlying hills of the area, it would be inappropriate not to devote a preliminary section to the Kennet & Avon Canal. Further, neither is this exclusively because of its remarkable history or current popularity (for a little more on these factors see below). Rather, it is because the canal passes through the Vale of Pewsey from one end to the other, offering glorious views of the downs, and providing vital and substantial links in a number of the walks. Were this not so, many of these walks could not be completed on a circular basis. But there are other benefits the canal provides, which merit a brief mention at this point. First, on wet and wild days when the downs are an impractical option, the canal offers a pleasant alternative to link delightful villages (see Wet Weather Alternatives, page 73). Second, access along the canal is excellent and continuous, thus a lovely countryside stroll does not grind to a halt when 'Bull in Field' signs or impassable mudbaths are encountered.

Constructed in the early 1800s, this canal boasts an interesting history. Bridging the gap between the rivers Kennet and Avon, a significant distance of some 57 miles, its completion was a triumph. However, it opened just as the railways were heralding the arrival of a totally new form of transportation, and before long therefore, fell into disrepair.

Its current popularity, as a pastime activity for canal boat enthusiasts and other tourists, is very much a recent phenomenon. In fact, only since the 1980s has the canal been fully navigable again, and this due to the tireless work of the Kennet and Avon Canal Trust, the charity set up by volunteers/enthusiasts to bring back to life this long dormant waterway.

Today, sections of the canal, perhaps especially the Caen Hill lock flight and the stretch between Bradford-on-Avon and Avoncliff, portray honey-pot characteristics during the summer months, and at weekends on an almost year round basis. However, the delightful stretch through the Vale of Pewsey, with which this guidebook is concerned, is pleasantly quiet, the towpath being unsuitable for bikes, and centres of any size besides the water, non-existent.

Combined with some superb views of the surrounding downland, it is perhaps not difficult to see why the canal hereabouts makes such a suitable link in several of the walks, as already noted.

Weather on the downs

Are you tired of heading to the mountains and upland regions of Britain, jaded by the hostility of the climate and what appears to be neverending rain, but are still searching for the thrill of bracing breezes and a real sense of being in the hills? If so, the Pewsey Downs are for you. Or perhaps you've never climbed a British mountain and have no real intention of doing so, but would like to experience a climate a little more challenging than that of typical lowland lanes and meadows. If so, then once again these downs will match your aspirations.

Lying at an altitude that never exceeds 300 metres above sea level (1,000 feet), but sitting proudly above the surrounding land, two distinct features are immediately significant. First, the climate is a lowland, not an upland one. Rainfall is remarkably moderate; on average just 33 inches of rain falls per year, that's less than most west facing, low lying regions of Britain, and only exceeds the driest regions by a few inches. In contrast, the Central and Western Beacons (South Wales) receive more than twice as much, while the highest ground of North Wales, the English Lake District and the Scottish Highlands, are notorious for particular wet spots, that in a bad year, are deluged with over 200 inches of moisture (although it does of course, come in a variety of forms – rain, sleet, snow, hail, mist etc)! So while the Pewsey Downs are green and verdant, few days over an extended period will be characterised by heavy rainfall, and even those that are, will be markedly less severe than wet days in upland regions.

Second, despite the moderate climate of the downs, their exposed position and relative elevation ensures they receive cooling breezes in the summer and bracing winds during the winter. The former temper high pressure, mid-summer days to splendid effect, producing conditions not dissimilar to those on coastal cliffs and headlands. The latter, when combined with rain, hail and/or occasional sleet, simulates an upland climate, but rarely if ever to the extreme that walkers are driven from the hills in fear for their safety. Experiencing such conditions, without the severe threat of exposure, represents a near perfect balance between adventure, unnecessary risk and miserable discomfort. Its one thing to experience strong winds a few moments from your car or a short distance away from the safety of the vale, its quite another to be reduced to a crawl (literally), on snow and ice, with zero visibility, high on some British mountain, hours from safety!

Besides these two endearing features of moderate rainfall and bracing winds, the downs have another significant characteristic in their favour – an excellent sunshine record! The tops of the downs actually receive considerably more sunshine than the Vale of Pewsey at their feet. Those who have walked in upland regions of Britain will note how special a blessing this is, for the pattern is completely reversed in true mountain regions, where to enjoy the sunshine its always better to keep to lower altitudes. This significant point is all the more poignant when considering that if these downs were barely 100 metres higher, they would be firmly in an upland category, and a sharp difference in climate statistics would be inevitable.

When to walk

As previously implied, the downs are attractive and safe for walkers, in all seasons. Thus, the question concerns the relative aesthetic merits they possess at different times of the year and, to some extent, the accompanying temperatures and available daylight.

Autumn is very hard to beat as the vale is set ablaze, when the turning leaves and low-lying sun combine to spectacular effect. Winter is rewarding for its semi-upland chill, occasional frosts and, often, superior visibility, as clear days and bare trees combine to produce distinct and uninterrupted views, both in the foreground and far distance. Spring produces a riot of colour as the yellow flowers of oil seed rape are among the bright colours which dominate the vale, while birds and other creatures herald the lengthening days and warming climate. Summer comes with its own charms too, as cooling breezes (during especially warm days at lower levels), can create an almost by-the-sea atmosphere. However, in early summer especially, vegetation can grow wildly, blocking footpaths and obscuring views, and causing considerable discomfort for those who are too scantily clad.

Don't restrict yourself to one or two seasons, but try them all. Seasonal climate variations enhance moderate, temperate zones, providing days of contrast that can produce memories to last a lifetime. Just ensure you are equipped appropriately for the time of year in question.

Equipment required

No one need spend a fortune kitting themselves out for walks (long or short) on these downs. However, a few basic principles, based on sound common sense, will add enjoyment to your day and lessen the risk of discomfort.

Warm and settled, mid-summer days apart, it is unwise to take to the higher tops without a waterproof coat, although a lightweight one of reasonable quality will probably suffice in almost all conditions, year-round. Lightweight boots with sufficient ankle support, good tread and effective cushioning are advisable at all times, especially during late autumn, winter and spring. Gloves and a hat will ensure vital body heat is conserved during cold, windy days, and a summer cap will shield you from some of the effects of strong sunshine. Otherwise, there is little to worry about, save the basic principle of wearing thin, man-made layers, that can be easily put on and removed, and which wick away sweat from the body, providing comfort in summer and preventing rapid cooling in winter when damp sweaty clothes can turn icily cold once a period of exertion comes to an end.

Maps, rights of way and access

Concerning all aspects of the heading above, we in Britain (England and Wales in particular), are privileged people indeed. The Ordnance Survey (OS) maps available – Landranger and Explorer – are of outstanding quality and enable walkers to venture forth with considerable confidence (providing they can read them), whether it be in lowland vales, on downland heights, over moors, along the coast or on the highest mountains. In addition, not only is the entire British mainland mapped in this way, we are even spoilt to the extent that we have a choice of map scales. The Landranger (1:50,000) is, in my view, the best series, because it ably balances sufficient detail with manageability while out on a walk; the maps being just small enough to fold neatly into a map holder, while providing enough information for the way ahead to be planned with care. However, they do not show field boundaries and are of necessity selective concerning the physical features included. Explorer maps, the larger scale alternative (1:25,000) do show field boundaries, and are wonderful for poring over in depth while planning and reflecting on a walk. So detailed are they in fact, that many a lovely walk can be relived, path by path, stile by stile and summit by summit. However, they are really too large to be conveniently carried on a walk, and as they are not cheap (£7.99 at time of going to print) it is worth bearing in mind that squeezed into a map holder, they are liable to tear, restricting their longevity considerably.

The best option, therefore, is probably to acquire both types of map, the Explorer for planning and reflection, the Landranger for use on the walks. This may appear extravagant, but as all the walks fit on just one map from each series (Landranger173 – Trowbridge and Devizes, Explorer 157 – Marlborough) it is a strategy well worth contemplating.

Moving on to rights of way and access, perhaps it has never struck you that the former are very much an English and Welsh phenomenon, for which every citizen should surely be permanently grateful. It is not a matter of small moment that we are legally permitted to pass through all manner of private land, safe in the knowledge that if we do so carefully and sensitively, we have no need to fear apprehension or aggression from landowners. How many of our fellow Europeans, or North American friends for that matter, would love to be able to do the same in their country? The myriad rights of way that exist, combined with additional open access areas (substantially increased since the 2000 Countryside Act and including Scotland also) provide us with comprehensive access to the

British countryside, sometimes in a manner that enable mile upon mile of walking to be enjoyed continuously.

The Pewsey Downs region specifically is no exception, general access being almost everywhere, excellent. Rights of way, By-ways, open downland access and quiet lanes (not to mention the towpath beside the Kennet & Avon Canal) provide a plethora of opportunities to gain an intimate understanding of this very special area. And if that were not enough, DEFRA currently have a farm conservation scheme in operation, in agreement with land owners, that enables additional access to be enjoyed in downland areas not strictly accessible via existing rights of way. These are due to expire in 2013 but nevertheless compliment already generous access rights and opportunities. The twelve walks in this guidebook make use of all the above access options, though not on an evenly distributed basis. Were this not the case, the walks would be fewer in number or of inferior quality.

Access is also very good in that one can start and finish all kinds of walks – long, short, strenuous and easy going – at very convenient points, close to villages, discrete roadside car parks and even some bus stops.

There is little that needs to be added at this point, other than to say that the maps included in this guidebook are there to provide a general overview of the walks and area covered, and should not therefore be used as a substitute for the OS maps discussed and described above.

Using the guide

The main intention of this guidebook is unambiguous. However, whether it is achieved is very firmly in yours, the reader's hands. It is to share my love of the Pewsey Downs and surrounding area in a manner that encourages you to edge forward a little in your armchair, reaching for your walking boots, casting your eyes over the bookshelf for the relevant map (if you possess it) and planning, with a keen sense of anticipation, an excursion in the not-too-distant future. If that objective can be occasionally achieved then that will be reason enough for completing this labour of love.

On a more practical note, in my view, any guidebook that simply offers instructions (however accurate and precise) is too mechanical, and can fail to inspire the wavering walker to head for the hills and vales. Therefore, I have deliberately embellished the preliminary sections with descriptive aspects in an attempt to inspire. Further, the walks themselves are just as deliberate a combination of clear directions and light-touch descriptive narrative; I sincerely hope this meets with your approval and taste.

All the walks start and finish at the same point, and ten of them are circular, while the remaining two are of an out-and-back nature. Concerning length, walks purposefully vary considerably, the shortest taking little more than an hour, the longest probably four times as long. Thus, there should be something for everyone, including outdoor fanatics, casual ramblers, families and mature citizens alike. The beauty of the Pewsey Downs is their tremendous diversity and versatility, providing wonderfully exciting excursions for every type of walker.

Each walk begins with a summary which should be sufficient to provide you with an overview, along with some genuine encouragements to seriously contemplate embarking on it. Parking and refreshment options are always mentioned too, even if they are in short supply.

It probably won't have escaped your attention that a number of the walks overlap at some point or another. However, this is quite deliberate, and not just because the area covered in the guidebook is relatively small and concentrated. Rather, it is because some of the finest points and features are worth visiting from quite different aspects on walks striking in their distinction. In fact, I myself confess that preparing this guidebook, and walking all over the region, including in areas I had previously ignored, has enabled me to gain a completely new perspective of the landscape hereabouts. Even the most familiar spots can be refreshingly different when approached from an entirely new direction. It has been a personal story of 'the more I have seen, the more I have discovered there is yet to be seen'. Where once I perhaps pictured the downs in a one-dimensional manner, now, in my mind's eye, I have a complex three-dimensional image, which I can recall with great pleasure, during quiet moments of reflection. I sincerely hope that, after completing some of these walks, you too will share this view and experience.

Finally, the guide has been written and designed to be taken on the walks but, if you are like me, you may be reluctant to get it out in all but the least threatening conditions. Do therefore, ensure you study it beforehand, and carry a map with you at all times.

Getting to/from the area

It will probably come as no surprise that those with their own car will be best placed to access the region and each of the walks in this guidebook. Further, as this part of the county is sparsely populated, and small, discrete parking areas quite plentiful, there is good reason to emphasize the benefits of accessing and getting around the area in this way. In addition, having your own car will maximise your flexibility concerning when and where you walk, and will enable the keen and energetic to complete more than one walk in a day or half day for that matter.

That said, for those without their own transport, there is good access to the region and, as mentioned above, as the walks are in quite a concentrated area, if you are reasonably fit, it should prove possible to walk to and from start points, by extending your walking plans a little.

The various bus services available represent the best form of public transport for accessing the walks. In fact, despite a lack of frequency on some routes, both the north and south of the downs can be accessed from west to east and at either extremes one can also use buses to travel south to north.

Devizes, Pewsey and Marlborough all serve as excellent gateways to the downs, the former two actually being within walking distance for those who have not been able to arrive in the region at a time to connect with a bus to match their plans. Even Calne serves as a potential gateway for walkers wishing to explore either the western downs or walks to the north, starting in East Kennett.

Advantageously, Pewsey has a mainline train station, enabling walkers to access the area from well beyond the confines of the Wessex region. With this thought in mind, one could quite reasonably contemplate a walking holiday in the region, using Pewsey as the gateway and then selecting either one base for accommodation (Pewsey, Oare, Honeystreet or Devizes would all be suitable) or roaming the area, using a variety of accommodation options.

To obtain the most up-to-date information, the best place to start is one of the local TICs, there being none more comprehensive in terms of information provision and opening times, than Devizes (01380 729408). Marlborough (01672 515190) and Avebury (01672 539425) will also be able to help, but Devizes is the senior centre for the Kennett region.

Country Code

It goes without saying that all walkers should familiarise themselves with the Country Code and adhere to it rigorously. To do so is not arduous but, rather, a simple display of gratitude and due care, for the wonderful environments we in Britain are privileged to enjoy legal access to.

The code is listed below and I would just add two further thoughts: first, these downs are not suitable for dogs unless kept under the strictest control, due to the number of free roaming sheep encountered; and second, try to avoid walking in large groups, to minimise the risk of disturbing livestock and wildlife, and to ensure maximum benefit from each and every walk.

- Guard against all risk of fire
- Fasten all gates
- Keep dogs under control
- Keep to public footpaths across farmland, and avoid taking short cuts which cause erosion
- Use gates and stiles to cross fences, hedges and walls
- Leave livestock, crops and machinery alone
- Take your litter home
- Help to keep all water clean
- Protect wildlife, plants and trees
- Take special care on country roads
- Make no unnecessary noise

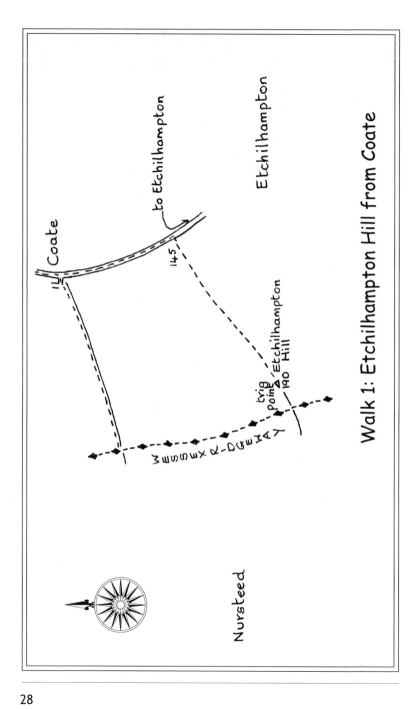

Walk 1: Etchilhampton Hill from Coate

Walk 1: Etchilhampton Hill from Coate

▲ *Start/Finish:* Coate
▲ *Distance:* 3.25 miles ~ 5.2km
▲ *Parking:* Parking area beside the cricket ground, in the centre of the village
▲ *Refreshment Options:* The New Inn
▲ *Walk Summary:* A short, circular walk that provides the perfect introduction to the Pewsey Downs. While not a part of the downs (being an isolated, outlying hill), views on approach to and from the summit take in the entire downland scene, from Roundway Hill in the west to Giant's Grave in the east
▲ *Suitable for:* All walkers, being brief and without steep sections, although a short, minor road section should be passed with care

Leave the village, heading south, via the road to Etchilhampton, noting almost immediately views of the Pewsey Downs to your L. Continue along the road for about half a mile (more of a quiet lane really, but one that should still be passed with due care and attention). Just before you leave the road, you will notice a slight incline and then your arrival on the brow of the hill. Turn R here onto a bridleway, via a gate.

Your grassy track now begins to ascend gently towards the summit of the hill offering pleasant views to the L and R. However, the finest views are behind you; thus, when you can bear the suspense no longer, a complete about-turn is recommended. The benign nature of this hill stands in marked contrast with the mouth-watering view of the downs now filling much of your horizon.

At your leisure, turn your back on the downs once more and continue uphill, heading for the soon-to-be-spotted trig point and summit. At 190m and with summit to vale differentials of little more than 50 metres, this hill is no giant but the view amply compensates. Arcing round from L to R is the whole of the Pewsey

Downs with a unique view of Roundway Hill thrown in for good measure, although from this angle, separating the latter from the former appears an artificial exercise.

When you have drunk your fill of this delightful spot, prolonging it on good days no doubt with time for photography, picnicking and downland summit spotting, continue west-south-west (with the distinct Westbury Chimney directly ahead of you) to reach, in a few moments, a track. Turn R here. When you reach a cross track, turn R and follow this back to the edge of the village, noting a quite different view of the hill to your R and more views of the Pewsey Downs ahead of you.

Primrose, a plant commonly
seen on downland slopes

Walk 2: Woodborough Hill from Alton Barnes

- ▲ *Start/Finish:* Alton Barnes
- ▲ *Parking:* Various points in Alton Barnes
- ▲ *Distance:* 3.5 miles ~ 5.6km
- ▲ *Refreshment Options:* The Barge Inn, Honeystreet
- ▲ *Walk Summary:* A short, out-and-back walk, to the summit of a beautiful, outlying hill, offering superb views of the downs, which are concealed until the summit is attained
- ▲ *Suitable for:* All walkers, being brief and without steep sections, but note there is a brief stretch of quiet road walking to be carefully negotiated at the start and finish of the walk

Begin by turning L onto the road you used to access the village, and follow it briefly to the bridge over the canal, which falls within the tiny settlement of Honeystreet.

Join the canal to the L (east), but note that, to do so, you must turn R onto the towpath to pass under the bridge, before proceeding. Immediately there are some magnificent views of the downs to be enjoyed.

Continue along the canal past the first bridge reached, to a second one. Note the gentle southern slopes of Woodborough Hill, leading away from the bridge on the opposite side of the canal.

Cross the bridge and forsake the canal to ascend the hill, which is now straight ahead of you. Pass farm outbuildings and climb easily to the summit. Be patient as you complete the climb as Woodborough jealously guards its panoramic hilltop views until the last possible moment. If visibility is good to excellent on the day of your walk, the summit views will be unforgettable, so be prepared to be detained for some time.

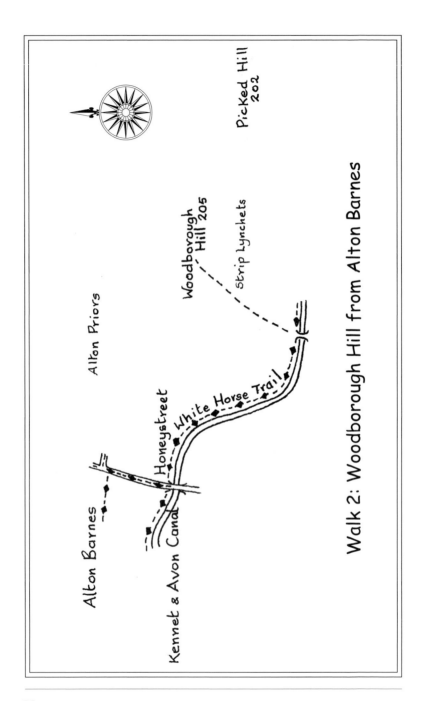

Picked Hill
202

Woodborough
Hill 205

Strip Lynchets

Alton Priors

Honeystreet

White Horse Trail

Alton Barnes

Kennet & Avon Canal

Walk 2: Woodborough Hill from Alton Barnes

When you can finally drag yourself away, return via your route of ascent to rejoin the canal, and then as you stroll back along it to Honeystreet, you will have time aplenty to ponder those summit views, plan a return trip and contemplate your next walk.

Return along the road for a few moments to complete this brief but delightful outing.

Note that, after returning to the towpath from the summit of Woodborough Hill, you can continue along the canal eastwards to the foot of beautiful Picked Hill that offers no legal access to its summit. However as you approach its base, the urge to climb it may be irresistible, thus it might be better to turn your back on it after all.

The canal towpath offers rewarding views en route to Woodborough Hill

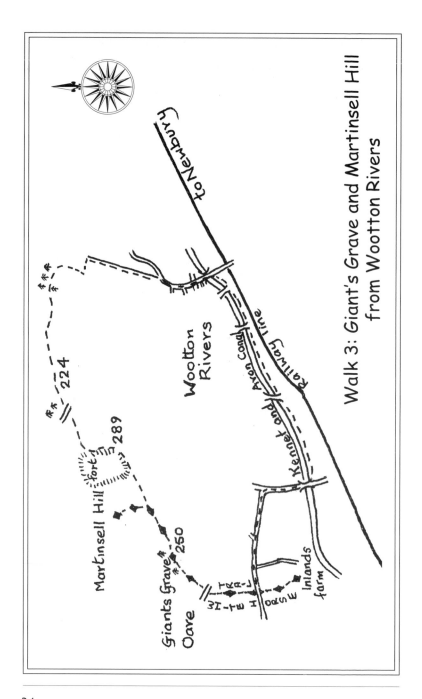

Walk 3: *Giant's Grave and Martinsell Hill from Wootton Rivers*

Walk 3: Giant's Grave and Martinsell Hill from Wootton Rivers

▲ *Start/Finish:* Wootton Rivers
▲ *Parking:* Southern end of the village, just north of the bridge over the canal. Alternatively the walk could be commenced from the car park at the foot of Martinsell Hill, that can be located beside the quiet country road, connecting Wootton Rivers with the A345 to the north-east
▲ *Distance:* 7.25 miles ~ 11.6km
▲ *Refreshment Options:* The Royal Oak, Wootton Rivers and the White Hart, Oare; the latter being literally moments from the route, where it reaches the track at the foot of Giant's Grave
▲ *Walk Summary:* A walk of surprising diversity and contrast, which begins with one of the finest stretches along the canal in these parts, followed by some pleasant and very quiet lane walking, with the Martinsell to Giant's Grave ridge filling the horizon to the north. Then an exhilarating ascent up to Giant's Grave precedes a roof top stroll out to Martinsell Hill. Finally, a descent to a wooded track and field completes the walk and leads back to Wootton Rivers
▲ *Suitable for:* Those seeking an extended walk of contrasts, and who can cope with a steep and strenuous ascent

Begin the walk at the bridge over the canal, turning R to join the towpath, trying to actively remember the number of bridges you pass under, as this will help to ensure you leave the canal at the right point. This is a lovely stretch of the towpath, and shortly you will have Martinsell Hill as your more-or-less constant companion to the north (R), as if to beckon you onwards and upwards.

Soon after joining the towpath two bridges are passed (both

quaint, rural ones with no road access). As you continue, note that the next bridge carries a quiet country lane over the canal. At this point you have passed under three bridges and will be leaving the towpath when the next one is reached.

When you reach the fourth bridge, leave the canal to the R on a lane, and head directly north, noting the Martinsell ridge ahead of you. Upland summiteers will no doubt have already observed the immense appeal of the Martinsell to Giant's Grave ridge, but now its magnetism will be obvious to all, especially if the day is fair and visibility good.

Looking east from Giant's Grave

When shortly you come to a turning on the L into another lane, follow it, forsaking the route ahead, and continue past farm houses and buildings for a little more than half a mile. When you reach a track and sign for Inlands Farm, continue on the lane but be ready to leave it imminently, to the R. This R hand turn is onto a grassy track at the field edge and, once on it, you are heading for Giant's Grave. As you draw closer to the foot of this hill, its aesthetic qualities become ever more obvious and compelling; note in particular how the ridge climbs into the sky in one graceful sweep.

When you reach a track, cross it and continue straight on, through a little gate and into the next field, heading for the field edge where its juts out slightly. Immediately after, cross a stile and then gird up your loins for one of the finest ascents in Wiltshire! Once on the summit of this remarkable hill, the immense panorama will amply repay, many times over, every ounce of effort required to attain it.

Continue along the ridge with the fence to your L and stay high to enjoy uninterrupted views, above slopes that tumble away steeply to the south, and towards the Vale of Pewsey carrying the canal beside which you recently strolled.

After passing through a small cluster of trees (and to the R of a stile and gate), where soon after a clear footpath leads down off the hill, continue eastwards, still maintaining your height and keeping the fence to your L. Eventually, after passing through a small area of gorse, you will reach a small gate on your L (Mid-Wilts Way – MWW – sign) besides a larger one straight ahead. Note also an open, flat field the other side of the fence, and another small, wooded area ahead. Pass through the small gate (on L), but continue in the same direction (east), following the path in and out of the trees to emerge within spying distance of a hill top bench on your R. Just beyond the bench is a gate leading onto Martinsell Hill, from where the view out over Eastern Wiltshire and Berkshire has to be seen to be believed!

Continue north along Martinsell's crest before dropping off to the east, down a surprisingly gentle spur, that always remains higher than the foot of the hill. Head for the parking area clearly visible from the hill's crest. When you reach it, cross the adjacent lane and join a track through the trees, appropriately named Mud Lane! This next stretch of the walk can be arduous in boggy conditions, but periodically to your L you will see little wooden posts that are conveniently numbered. The first you will come to is numbered

15W. When you have passed 1W prepare to leave the lane to the R, noting the MWW signpost which guides you to the precise point of departure.

Continue beside the field edge, and when you reach the corner of the field turn L. Shortly you will come to a grassy downhill track on the R, with trees on either side: follow it down into Wootton Rivers, the village where this lovely walk began.

When the track reaches the village, continue straight on, passing a delightful diversity of dwellings to return to your starting point.

Please note: When you reach Mud Lane, if it looks especially boggy and you fear slogging along the muddy track may tarnish an otherwise enjoyable walk, consider following the quiet country lane from the car park to Wootton Rivers instead. If you are tempted, turn R onto the road and follow it downhill, then turn L to pass beside East Wick Farm, and continue along the lane down into the village.

The views of Martinsell Hill, first on your R and then later behind you, are so impressive and the lane so pleasantly quiet, that it is tempting to choose the alternative on all occasions, rather than just when the weather and underfoot conditions are inclement. But then again, variety and choice are pleasant aspects of many a walk in the countryside.

Lark, whose song you may hear on a summer's day on the downs

Walk 4: A high level circuit above the village of Oare

▲ *Start/Finish & Parking:* Small, concealed parking area (5-6 car capacity), immediately adjacent to the A345, on the brow of the hill north of the village of Oare. (Note that a sign forbidding vehicular access applies to the lane beyond the parking area, and not the parking area itself)

▲ *Please note:* For those arriving by bus, the village serves as an equally good starting point. If wanting to park in the village, it would be wise to phone the pub in advance to ask for permission to park there, although there is a small on-street parking area just prior to the bus stop.

▲ *Distance:* 4 miles ~ 6.4km

▲ *Refreshment Options:* The White Hart, Oare

▲ *Walk Summary:* It is hard to imagine a more dramatic, action packed circular walk over so short a distance, than this one! After a gentle start, the arrival and views from Martinsell Hill are unforgettable. Then the panorama from Giant's Grave and descent from the same is equally dramatic. And if that were not sufficient drama already, the ascent up out of Oare is very steep and the views yet again delightful. A gentle stroll along the top of the downs then leads back to your starting point

▲ *Suitable for:* Most walkers, but the steep ascent referred to (albeit short-lived) may render it beyond the limits of those whose fitness has waned of late, or who have indulged in too hearty a lunch at the White Hart, in Oare village

Head east along the track, leading from the parking area, on a slight uphill gradient until you reach a gate across the path,

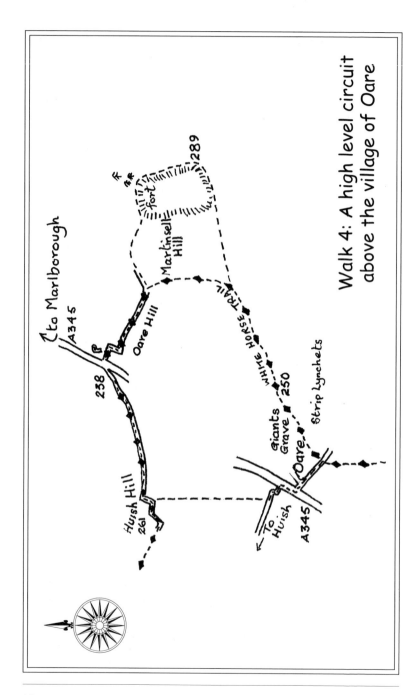

Walk 4: A high level circuit above the village of Oare

leading to an open field. Turn L here to enter a narrow, wooded area, which can become boggy during winter months and after prolonged wet spells at other times of the year.

Continue through the trees, eventually emerging (shortly after a signed footpath crossroads) to enjoy a spectacular view north, out over the seemingly endless Marlborough Downs. Keep the fence to your R and soon you will reach the summit crest of Martinsell Hill, without doubt one of the region's finest viewpoints.

Turn R and wander along the crest, where the combination of steep slopes and far-reaching panorama make for dramatic and compelling viewing!

When you reach a gate at the southern end of the crest, where the downs turn west at a right angle, pass through it, noting a conspicuous bench on your L. Now pass through a small wooded area, keeping the fence to your L. When you emerge from the trees, spy a gate a few metres in front of you. Pass through it, but stay high on the downs, keeping the fence to your immediate R.

Looking north over the Marlborough Downs

Continue westwards – noting how the entire Vale of Pewsey is opening up before you – to arrive eventually atop Giant's Grave, an ancient hill top burial ground of advantageous elevation. Once again the views all around are mesmerising. When you reach a trig point, the hill plunges to the valley floor in one clean, breathtaking sweep; here one feels almost aerial.

Drop off the hill via the aforementioned slopes and arc round to the L, via the field edge, to reach a stile. Cross it and head south (straight on) to reach a gate clearly visible ahead, that leads onto a track. Turn R onto the track and follow it into the village of Oare, taking care as you cross the A345.

Turn R after crossing the road and pass the White Hart on your L (or pop in for a bite to eat if it's lunchtime). Very soon after, turn L onto a lane, signposted to Huish. When you pass a row of pretty cottages on your R and a school to your L, turn R into a field with the downs looming large ahead of you. Follow the field edge to reach a gate at the foot of the downs.

Having prepared yourself for a stiff ascent, head straight up onto the downs, noting a bench near the top, beautifully positioned to reward the climber and those in search of a delectable view. Then continue directly uphill, ignoring gates to the L and R, to reach one at the very top. Pass through it and continue ahead, noting mature trees to your L.

Follow the path and shortly join a track, turning R onto it. Stay on this track all the way to the road (A345), which should again be crossed with particular care. Soon after, you will spot your car, just a few metres ahead of you.

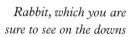

Rabbit, which you are
sure to see on the downs

Walk 5: The downland crest between Knap Hill and Oare

▲ *Start/Finish & Parking:* Knap Hill Car Park, north of Alton Barnes, on the brow of the hill between Walker's Hill and Knap Hill

▲ *Distance:* 7 miles ~ 11.2km

▲ *Refreshment Options:* White Hart, Oare

▲ *Walk Summary:* A prolonged, out-and-back walk along the crest of the downs between Knap Hill and Huish Hill, affording magnificent, unbroken views

▲ *Suitable for:* Older children and those who can manage a steep descent and re-ascent, as well as quite a long walk

Leave the car park heading for Knap Hill, noting immediately a fine view of Woodborough Hill and Picked Hill – classic, but non-identical twins. Cross a stile on the L to ascend Knap Hill by an easy path. The outstanding summit view sets the tone for the entire walk! Not only does the Vale of Pewsey draw the eye, but so too the remarkable steepness and shape of the downs hereabouts. In fact, many a mountain several times the height, would be put to shame by the profile of the surrounding, surprisingly independent, downland tops.

Follow the crest of the downs over a series of stiles to a wooded area that looms large ahead of you (Gopher Wood). Skirt this to the L, to reach a gate and stile. Now temporarily, the crest of the downs is forsaken but alternative views to the north amply compensate. Follow the edge of the field and wood downhill to another stile, and continue further downhill to reach a gate and cross-track, followed by another gate. Now you are back close to the crest of the downs which leads gently uphill. Keep close to this crest which is part of an open-access area.

After a period of delightful and elevated walking, spy a house to

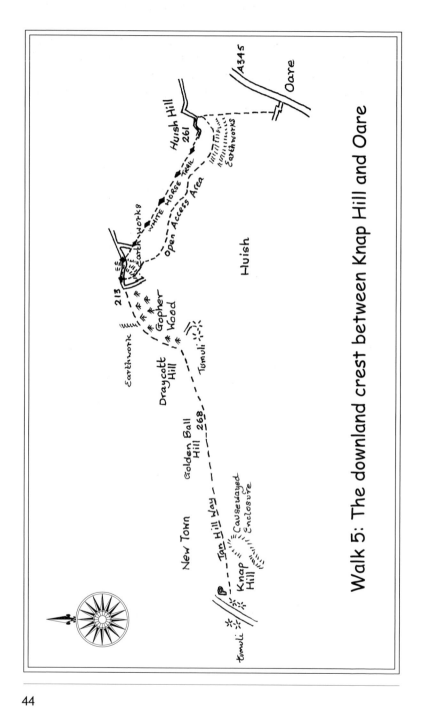

Walk 5: The downland crest between Knap Hill and Oare

your L (Huish Hill House), set some way back on the downland plateau and well to the other side of the fence now immediately beside you; now your descent is at hand (to aid you a little further, this is also the point where the downs arc round in a horseshoe shape ahead).

Pass through a gate and diagonally downhill, shortly reaching a bench, the top of which is just visible from the gate. This bench not only provides rest for those ascending the hill, but a poignant spot from which to admire and absorb the surrounding downland and vale scenery.

Head directly and steeply downhill to a gate and continue along the field edge to a lane on the edge of Oare village. Turn L and follow the lane to a junction in the village. Now turn R to reach in a few moments The White Hart pub – the ideal location for a spot of well deserved lunch.

Re-trace your route after lunch.

If carrying lunch with you, you may wish to devour it on the bench at the top of the steep hill, forsaking the descent and re-ascent and maximising hilltop viewing time.

The Pewsey Downs (seen here from Knap Hill) are a riot of individual hills jostling, quite rightly, for personal attention

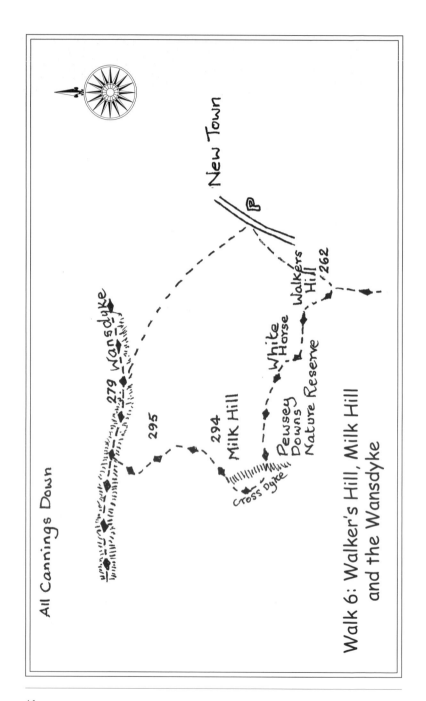

All Cannings Down

New Town

279 Wansdyke

295

294
Milk Hill

Cross Dyke

White
Horse

Pewsey
Downs
Nature Reserve

Walkers
Hill

262

Walk 6: Walker's Hill, Milk Hill
and the Wansdyke

Walk 6: Walker's Hill, Milk Hill and the Wansdyke

▲ *Start/Finish and Parking:* Knap Hill Car Park

▲ *Distance:* 3 miles ~ 4.8km

▲ *Refreshment Options:* None en route, but the Barge Inn, Honeystreet and the White Hart, Oare are only a few minutes drive away

▲ *Walk Summary:* A short, dramatic walk over high downland and along the Wansdyke, with bird's eye views, and on wintry days, a distinct upland flavour

▲ *Suitable for:* All walkers on warm spring, summer and autumn days as it is a brief walk without steep sections. However, as it traces high and exposed downland, on cold and wintry days it is not an ideal environment for young children or those inappropriately clad

Begin the walk leaving Knap Hill car park, via a L turn onto and across the road.

Continue along the grassy verge for just a few moments, heading in the direction of Walker's Hill, and cross a stile leading onto the downland. Make for another stile straight ahead of you and then turn L, heading directly for Walker's Hill. Cross one more stile and strike uphill for the pointy summit of this delightful perch.

On a clear day, the view to be enjoyed from the summit of this hill is another of Wiltshire's finest! Way to the east (L) Ham Hill and the Berkshire border can be easily identified, while to the south-west the Westbury Downs draw the eye, the chimney at their feet ensuring that the correct spot has been located. But peel the eyes and further south (but still westwards too), the most elongated Deverill ridge can be picked out. Brimsdown Hill and Cold Kitchen Hill (the prominent high points of this ridge) are no more than a few miles from Dorset, yet their shape and location, to them that know them intimately, is beyond doubt! Myriad other scenic splendours may well detain you for some time, not to mention the opportunity for a detailed study of the downs themselves, which can be viewed extensively in both directions.

Leave the summit to the west (R as you gaze out over the vale at your feet), soon passing the Alton Barnes White Horse, and then a hillside gate.

Follow the downs as they curve north in a smooth U-shape through two more gates, noting steep, dramatic slopes to your L (west). When you eventually reach a weighted gate, still high on the downs, pass through it and continue north to reach another one, shortly after.

Now join the Wansdyke and turn R (east) following along the northern fringes of Milk Hill, the highest (but not the most impressive) point in the county.

After a short but exhilarating stroll atop the dyke you will come to an obvious and quite steep break; branch R here (passing first through a gate to your L) on an obvious path that heads in a south-easterly direction, uphill for the first few metres, and with a fence to your R. Follow this all the way back to the car park – visible from some distance – and note the intriguing aspect of Walker's Hill and Knap Hill from the north, very much a 'from behind' view.

Roe Deer, more often to be seen in wooded areas

Walk 7: The Central Downs from Alton Barnes

▲ *Start/Finish:* Alton Barnes
▲ *Parking:* Various points in Alton Barnes (alternatively you could start the walk from Knap Hill car park)
▲ *Distance:* 8 miles ~ 12.8km
▲ *Refreshment Options:* King's Arms, All Cannings and the Barge Inn, Honeystreet
▲ *Walk Summary:* A wonderful combination of gentle canal walking, village exploration and bracing downland ascent, all washed down with visits to Wiltshire's two highest points and a memorable stretch along the Wansdyke
▲ *Suitable for:* Most walkers, although the ascent involved and the extended period on high ground, may place it beyond the bounds of young children and the less mobile
▲ *Please note:* There is a very brief but potentially tricky stretch of road to be negotiated, where the verges are quite steep, which should be passed in single file and with special care. Young children should be kept under the strictest supervision or taken on an alternative walk

Begin in the heart of this pretty village, heading in the direction of the superbly preserved St Mary Saxon Church (which will most likely be open and where regular services are still held). Before you reach it, enter the village green on your L, via an old fashioned, wooden turnstile, probably designed and constructed by the village carpenter from a bygone age. Now pass through the green via a diagonal, cobbled path, with the church a little way to your right. When soon presented with a choice of paths take the R option (straight on in effect), noting that you are now parallel with the church and heading towards another. Note also to your L,

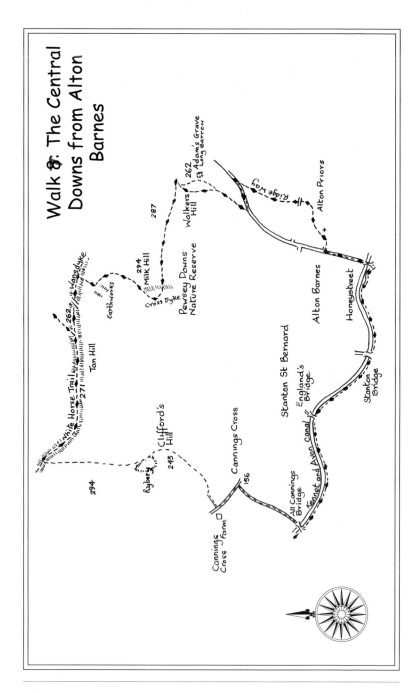

Walk 8: The Central Downs from Alton Barnes

- Adam's Grave Long Barrow
- 262
- Walkers Hill
- Ridge Way
- Alton Priors
- 287
- Milk Hill
- 294
- Cross Dyke
- Pewsey Downs Nature Reserve
- Wansdyke
- 262
- White Horse Trail
- Earthworks
- Tan Hill
- 271
- Alton Barnes
- Honeystreet
- Stanton St Bernard
- England's Bridge
- Stanton Bridge
- Rybury
- Clifford's Hill
- 245
- 294
- Cannings Cross
- Cannings Cross Farm
- All Cannings Bridge
- 156
- Kennet and Avon Canal

Walker's Hill, a compelling sight and your first major objective on this walk.

Pass over two adjacent little bridges and through two more wooden turnstiles and to the L of a second church (you have now seamlessly passed into Alton Priors), to reach a lane which you follow to the L to continue. Soon after you come to a T-junction, where there is a stunning thatched outbuilding to your L, a pleasing, rural touch. Cross the road with care and join an uphill track-cum-path. After a few seconds take a R to continue uphill along the field edge. Follow this path until you reach the road, some way uphill. On arrival at the road, you have no option but to join it, turning L and heading downhill for a few moments. While this is not a main road, and is also the route of a waymarked long distance trail – the White Horse Trail – you should take special care. Here, the verges are steep and the road quite narrow without an extended clear line of vision. It takes only a few brief moments to negotiate, but vigilance is necessary to avoid incident.

*A wooden turnstile in Alton Barnes – a village
in the vale where time stands still*

Just before a bend there is a signed path on the opposite side, which leads uphill. Follow this and note, immediately, the downland drama, Walker's Hill beckoning you onward and upward. Pass through a gate and continue uphill to the summit of the hill, on a pleasantly aesthetic spur.

Enjoy the extraordinary summit views, which feature the entire breadth of the county, before continuing west beyond Alton Barnes White Horse (not very white actually, but visible from miles around nevertheless) and then through a hillside gate. Then as you reach the southern fringes of Milk Hill, follow the scarp edge as it arcs round to the north. While the exact highest point of the Milk Hill plateau is out of sight and beyond reach at this point, your position and views west are captivating! Steep slopes tumble to the valley floor, and just beyond, Tan Hill and Clifford's Hill present a bold and arresting front. On warm and calm days (of which in the summer months there are many), this would be a fine spot in which to enjoy a leisurely packed lunch, while pouring over the view and picking out various points of interest.

Continue north through two gates to a third, weighted gate (still high on the downs and towards the end of the U-shaped curve of the scarp edge) and pass through it, heading straight on (north) to reach another one in a few minutes. Turn L here to join the Wansdyke. This is one of the finest sections of the dyke, so enjoy it to the full, noting how its elevated character provides a superior viewpoint.

When the dyke starts to trail north-west (on the fringes of Tan Hill) strike south, south-west (L) keeping the summit hilltop fence to your R. Just besides the fence, but on the other side, you will notice the trig point.

Continue south through a gate and head downhill, into the dip between Tan Hill and Clifford's Hill. Here as much as anywhere on these downs one really could be in an upland environment (excluding the climate of course), the sense of seclusion being almost tangible.

Pass through another gate and head quite steeply uphill to the twin summits of Clifford's Hill. Here again the panorama awaiting you and hill top ambience are awe inspiring.

Conclude the downland stretch of this walk heading south, south-west (straight ahead), and by descending the spur of this remarkable hill. Scenic drama accompanies you in all directions until height is finally lost. When, at the foot of the hill you reach some gates, pass through them and continue along the track to the roadside. Turn L when you reach it and make use of the generous verge. Shortly turn R onto the road leading to All Cannings.

When you cross a little bridge over the canal, turn immediately L to join the towpath, and follow it east to Honeystreet. This leisurely finish represents the ideal way to savour your recent exploits, enjoy the downland views and warm down.

Just before you reach the road, the towpath passes right beside the Barge Inn; surely a fitting place in which to reward your tired limbs.

On reaching the road, turn L and follow it for a few minutes, to return to Alton Barnes.

Alton Priors' tiny church – a stone's throw from the Saxon church in Alton Barnes

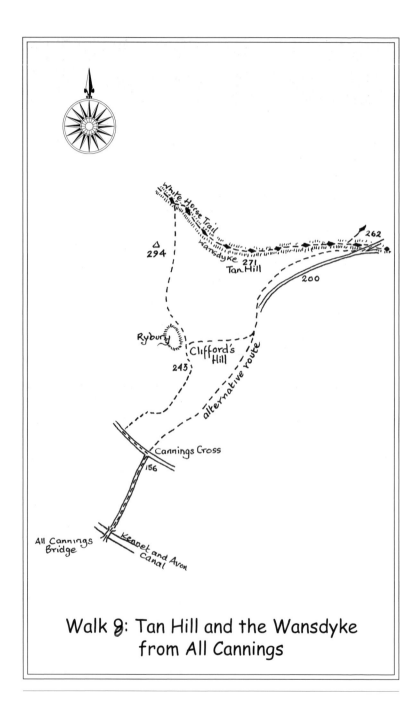

White Horse Trail

262

△ 294

Wansdyke 271
Tan Hill

200

Rybury
Clifford's Hill

245

alternative route

Cannings Cross

156

All Cannings
Bridge

Kennet and Avon
Canal

Walk 9: Tan Hill and the Wansdyke
from All Cannings

Walk 8: Tan Hill and the Wansdyke from All Cannings

▲ *Start/Finish:* All Cannings
▲ *Parking:* Car park beside the Kennet & Avon Canal to the north of the village
▲ *Distance:* 5.5 miles ~ 8.8km
▲ *Refreshment Options:* The King's Arms, All Cannings
▲ *Walk Summary:* An unbeatable walk offering semi-upland thrills, breathtaking views and generally easy walking. The route of ascent is dramatic and arresting, as it provides stunning views from the moment height is gained, ahead, behind and to the L & R
▲ *Suitable for:* Most walkers, but should perhaps be avoided by those who struggle with sustained ascents. On wintry days, young children may also find it beyond their comfort zone

To begin, turn R onto the road leading from the car park and cross the canal bridge. Note the downs, dominating the scene ahead. When you reach the T-junction, cross the road, turn L and pass with care for a few moments along the grassy verge taking a track on the right besides Cannings Cross Farm. When shortly you reach three gates, pass through either the smaller, central one or the right- hand one and head up onto the downs. Already a remarkable view begins to open out; Etchilhampton Hill, Roundway Hill, Morgan's Hill and much of the Pewsey Downs ridge compete for your attention, and this just minutes after the start of the walk! As the breeze stiffens and the ground falls away sharply to your L (west), the sense of drama is palpable.

Keeping fences to your R, continue ascending to the summit of Clifford's Hill. Here again the scenery in all directions will no doubt detain you but, to continue, walk in a north-westerly direction towards the Tan Hill plateau, enjoying the undulating ridge in the process. After a fairly steep but brief descent, the final ascent to Tan Hill commences, immediately after passing through a little gate.

When you reach the Tan Hill plateau, head north to join the Wansdyke, noting the Tan Hill trig point, the other side of a fence to your L. For the second highest point in Wiltshire this may come as an anti-climax! Tan Hill is not a pointy summit, but rather just the highest point on a plateau of considerable size. This provides a valuable lesson, if one is needed, that height alone is never a good criterion on which to base any assessment of a hill's merits and aesthetic qualities. That said, the view hereabouts is marvellous, more than compensating for any disappointment.

Looking down Clifford's Hill's southern spur to All Cannings and Etchilhampton Hill

As you join the dyke, turn R (east) and follow it for about a mile. This dyke is a ridge in miniature, and combined with the height of the downs makes for a stirring and elevated section of the walk.

When a surfaced track crosses the dyke, turn R onto it and head downhill. Almost immediately an opportunity arises to join a grassy, parallel path, via a gate, which is much to be preferred to the track (now a narrow, private but fully surfaced road). On reaching the valley floor, the track is rejoined beside a farm outbuilding.

Continue along the track, but soon take a R, through a gate, to re-ascend Clifford's Hill, this time via its east ridge. On reaching the summit turn L (south), and retrace your opening steps to regain the road leading back to the canal, on the edge of All Cannings.

Please note: If the idea of re-ascending Clifford's Hill sounds over zealous and eccentric, there is an easy but second best alternative, via a track which leaves the farm track immediately after the gate leading uphill; but don't complain of inferior views or any sense of anti-climax as the walk draws to a close and you spy walkers dropping off the downs and the path you spurned, cooing over the extensive views, as they gaze south over the Vale of Pewsey.

Fox, always thrilling to see, if only for a moment

White Horse Trail

Wansdyke

Bourton

Bishop Cannings

Horton

Kennet and Avon Canal

133

Allington
163

White Horse Trail

All Cannings
Bridge

156

Clifford's
Hill

△ 294

All Cannings

Walk 9:
The Western Downs
from
Bishop's Cannings

All Cannings Church

Walk 9: The Western Downs from Bishop's Cannings

▲ *Start/Finish:* Bishop's Cannings
▲ *Parking:* Various points in Bishop's Cannings, including a substantial parking area on the fringes of the village, when approaching from the A361 (west)
▲ *Distance:* 8.75 miles ~ 14km
▲ *Refreshment Options:* The Crown Inn, Bishop's Cannings, The King's Arms, All Cannings
▲ *Walk Summary:* A superbly varied walk of ceaseless interest and excitement, combining a gentle start along the canal, a thrilling ascent onto the downs, a stretch across the roof of Wiltshire, a prolonged spell atop the Wansdyke and the kindest of descents back down into Bishop's Cannings
▲ *Suitable for:* Those walkers who like a sustained outing of tremendous variety, without too much strenuous activity. Young children, unless exceptionally keen, will probably complain that the walk is too long, from about the half-way point onwards

Take the second R after entering the village from the A361 (west) and follow the lane to the edge of the village. En route note the sign to Bishop's Cannings' delightful church - St. Mary the Virgin - which sits amidst the most picturesque surroundings. The church will almost certainly be open and is kept in impeccable condition and would be well worth a visit when you have completed the walk.

When you reach the lane end, pass through a kissing gate - noting an excellent view of the Pewsey Downs to your L - and continue on a road surfaced track. In a few moments you will reach the canal which is crossed via a bridge.

Turn L as you join the towpath and follow it all the way to the bridge and road leading to/from All Cannings (where Walk 8 begins). Leave the canal here, turning L to follow the road north, to a T-junction. Turn L, cross the road and follow the wide, grassy verge for a few moments until you reach a track beside Cannings Cross Farm. Turn R onto the track and follow it to some gates, passing through the middle or right hand of three possible options. Now continue uphill enjoying one of the finest ascents in the Pewsey Downs. The sense of drama and excitement hereabouts is tangible, Clifford's Hill's twin summits beckoning, and Wiltshire's highest ground towering ahead and to the R (Tan Hill and Milk Hill).

The route drops briefly but steeply just after Clifford's Hill's second summit, but then the climb to the Tan Hill plateau begins. Pass through a gate and head uphill. As the hill flattens out another gate is reached, after which the path continues straight on besides a fence (to your L). Note in a short while the trig point situated on the highest part of Tan Hill and just the other side of the fence.

Continue directly north to reach the Wansdyke and join it at a small breach, via a gate. Turn L onto it and head west. The blend of superb scenery, quiet solitude and historical perspective is remarkable!

Continue along the dyke, over a cross track (signposted to Townsend Farm) and past a farm outbuilding which, when combined with a few trees, temporarily hides the continuing path.

Soon you will reach another cross track. Continue, but note that a short distance ahead the dyke begins to rise: this is the point at which you will leave it. When you reach the next cross track signalling the gentle rise just mentioned, turn L onto it and continue gently downhill past another farm outbuilding.

Follow this pleasant track to an open, almost welcoming farmyard and then turn R onto a lane. Follow this lane, passing houses and a few turnings to reach the village and complete the walk.

Walk 10: The Wansdyke from East Kennett

▲ *Start/Finish:* East Kennett
▲ *Parking:* Various points in East Kennett
▲ *Distance:* 5.75 miles ~ 9.2km
▲ *Refreshment Options:* None en route but various options in villages nearby
▲ *Walk Summary:* An almost secretive approach to the Pewsey Downs and Wansdyke from the north, through very pleasant countryside. When views of various downland hills and the Vale of Pewsey suddenly fill the horizon, an entirely different aspect is revealed, adding a new dimension to the walk. Then the passage along the Wansdyke provides more far reaching views in both directions, before you leave it to descend gently to the valley floor, returning to East Kennett and your starting point
▲ *Suitable for:* Most walkers, however the length of the walk, combined with exposure to cold winds on wintry days, may place it beyond the capabilities of young children

Head along the village road which trends south-east and then south, noting the lovely cottages all around. Just as you leave the village take a R fork onto a By-way passing a sign for East Kennett Manor Farm.

In a short while, leave the main track to take a rising, grassy alternative on your L (also a By-way), which runs parallel to the track you previously followed. As you gain height the landscape begins to open up offering lovely views of quiet downland countryside.

Continue uphill into a small wooded area, but be warned, during winter and after very wet spells, the track can be very muddy for

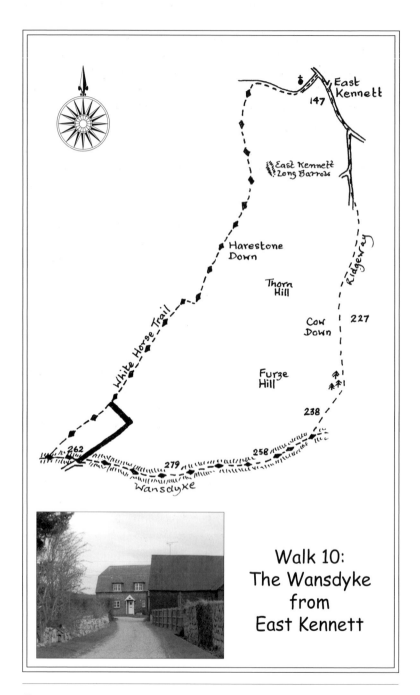

East Kennett

147

East Kennett Long Barrows

Harestone Down

Thorn Hill

Ridgeway

Cow Down

227

Furze Hill

238

White Horse Trail

262

279

258

Wansdyke

Walk 10:
The Wansdyke
from
East Kennett

a short while. Just as the boggy path becomes a little tiresome, you will emerge from the trees to be greeted by an unforgettable sight! This view of various downland summits and glimpses of the Vale of Pewsey (Knap Hill, Walker's Hill and Woodborough Hill all compete for your attention), might from this angle be termed 'Back of the Pewsey Downs'.

After admiring the view turn R and very soon join the unmistakeable Wansdyke. The views were already fine, but this lofty ridge-top perch, affords marvellous views of its own, and now in every direction.

Follow the dyke for a little over a mile, enjoying the contrasting landscapes, where to the L the downs' steep south-facing slopes and the vale provide drama and beauty, and to the R the peaceful plateau of the Marlborough Downs, a scene of unruffled tranquillity.

When you reach a clear cross track-cum-private road, with views of Clifford's Hill and Tan Hill some way ahead, and Milk Hill beside you to your L, your departure from the dyke is moments away. Cross the track and rejoin the dyke, but peel your eyes to the R, for a point in the fence where it can be unclipped (a slightly tricky manoeuvre). Now follow the track downhill, with another fence to your R, noting that shortly the cross track you recently encountered once again crosses your path.

Continue without complications, enjoying the pleasant scenery, noting one very brief R hand, uphill turn, until a cross track is reached on the fringes of East Kennett. Turn R here and follow it into the village, between farm buildings and past the charming church, noting the village dwellings to your L and R, some thatched, some tiled, all delightful.

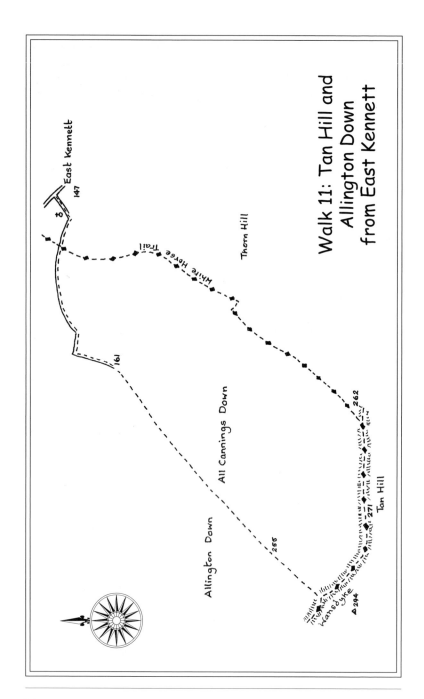

Walk 11: Tan Hill and Allington Down from East Kennett

East Kennett

147

White Horse Trail

Thorn Hill

161

All Cannings Down

Allington Down

255

262

271

Tan Hill

Wansdyke

294

Walk 11: Tan Hill and Allington Down from East Kennett

▲ *Start/Finish:* East Kennett
▲ *Parking:* Various points in East Kennett
Distance: 6.5 miles ~ 10.4km
▲ *Refreshment Options:* None en route but various options in villages nearby
▲ *Walk Summary:* A lovely approach walk to the Pewsey Downs and Wansdyke, followed by a high level stretch along the latter, affording wonderful views in all directions. Then a prolonged descent via Allington Down provides a stirring return to East Kennett
▲ *Suitable for:* Most walkers, however the length of the walk, combined with exposure to cold winds on wintry days, may place it beyond the capabilities of young children

Leave the main village road via a lane to the south-west, passing pretty cottages, the church and farm buildings to emerge onto a track which bears R soon after you join it. Then when you reach a cross track (and the White Horse Trail simultaneously), turn L and follow it gently uphill, all the way to the Wansdyke. (Note that the route of ascent is identical to the descent route used in walk 10.)

As you approach the Wansdyke, you may think that there is no break in the fence through which to access it, but peel your eyes and you will see a point at which the fence can be unclipped. Now clamber atop the dyke, turning R as you do so.

Follow the dyke west enjoying the airy, ridge-top position and perspective. Clifford's Hill and the Vale of Pewsey look especially pleasing, the former being sufficiently nearby to tempt one to embark on an unplanned, additional excursion to take in its superb summit views. But note also Etchilhampton Hill, simultaneously aesthetically pleasing and an isolated viewpoint of some note – which it most certainly is.

As you skirt Tan Hill to the north, twenty metres below the highest point (the trig point itself not visible) note your arrival at a gate and stile at a break in the dyke. Turn R here to leave the dyke and head in a north-east direction, on an obvious path-cum-track with a fence to your R.

Any sadness over leaving the dyke will soon be quickly forgotten as a very different aspect now arrests the attention. As well as some interesting retrospective views of the dyke, views west, east and north are stunning. West especially, Roundway Hill, Morgan's Hill and Cherhill Hill invite detailed study, but straight ahead too, the far reaching views of unspoilt downland are a delight. Further, the nature of the descent is such that mountaineers and upland wanderers everywhere would be green with envy, as it combines the easiest of gradients, kind terrain and sustained views.

Continue downhill, noting where the path becomes fenced on both sides, whereafter you soon reach a clear track. Follow it and continue over two cross tracks (the second of which was your route of ascent) to re-enter the village and, to return to your starting point.

The twin summits of Clifford's Hill from the Wansdyke

Walk 12: Roundway Hill, Morgan's Hill and the downs' western terminus

▲ *Start/Finish:* Roundway Hill

▲ *Parking:* Parking area near the top of Roundway Hill, after taking the R of two options where the road forks. Access to Roundway Hill is first via Devizes and then the little settlement of Roundway, from where a lane strikes north, at the point where the through road turns sharply to the L

▲ *Distance:* 8.5 miles ~ 13.6km

▲ *Refreshment Options:* None en route

▲ *Walk Summary:* An easy but sustained walk, taking in two superb hill top viewpoints (Morgan's Hill and Roundway Hill), beyond the accepted boundaries of the Pewsey Downs

▲ *Suitable for:* Most walkers as there are no steep ascents. However, the length of this walk may place it beyond the reach of those with young children

Just before beginning the walk, turn R as if to return the way you have just come, and walk a few steps to take in the view east, of Bishop's Cannings (its church spire being very prominent) and the Pewsey Downs. You might also note the Roundway Hill White Horse, just seconds away on the downland slopes, but difficult to pick out from a side-on angle.

Having studied the view, commence the walk to your L (north-east) from the parking area and head along the track. To your R is the summit of Roundway Hill – intriguing and very pleasing to the eye, but not nearly as dramatic as the scarp edge of Roundway Down, presently out of sight to the west. Note also straight ahead the twin masts sitting atop the summit of Morgan's Hill, one of this walk's principal objectives.

Continue on the track until you come to a cross-track. Turn R here; shortly after you come to a road which should be crossed with

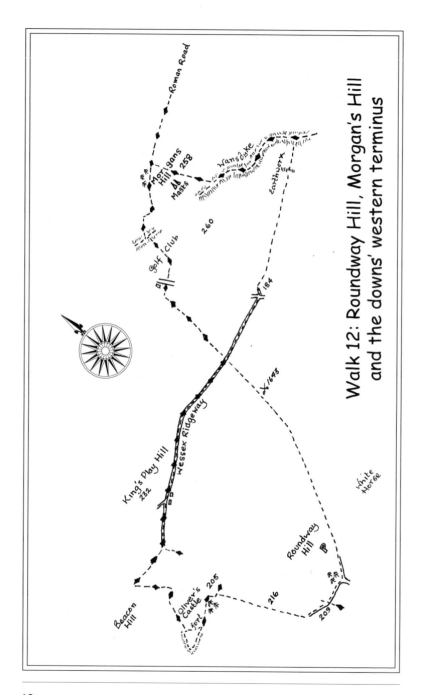

Walk 12: Roundway Hill, Morgan's Hill and the downs' western terminus

care. Continue on the track, noting that just after crossing the road, it bears to the R of four adjacent gates. As you progress, a few trees start to line the route.

Keep a lookout for the Wansdyke path to your R, clearly visible from some distance, especially in clear conditions. When you reach it, you simultaneously enter a continuous but small area of trees. You will then see a gate to your R, onto the Wansdyke, but at this point you need to turn L, off the track, and into and out of the trees, to join the Wansdyke heading west. Pass through a gate and onto the dyke enjoying superb views to the R (north), taking in the Cherhill Monument and the surrounding, uncultivated ground.

Soon you will reach a second gate but, this time, in a dip to the L of the dyke. After passing through it, you soon climb out of the dip, with the twin masts and Morgan's Hill immediately ahead of you.

Bear R on a feint track, passing well to the R of the masts, and make for the fence, following it to the far R hand corner, where a gate leads onto Morgan's Hill Nature Reserve. Turn L here and enjoy splendid views from yet another lovely hill top, but this time to the north, where Calne, Chippenham and more rural delights draw the eye and complete a varied scene.

Remain high as you traverse the hillside, and when you pass a bench look out for a gate on your L, leading onto North Wilts Golf Club. When you reach it, turn L and follow an obvious path which immediately turns R and leads gently downhill, with a fence to your L. When the fence turns L at a right angle, head straight on, noting occasional footpath signs. Pass through a small cluster of trees and head for the road and just to the L of the clubhouse, taking care not to stray into the path of any aerial golf balls. Cross the road with care (a long, fast and straight one) and join a track to the immediate L of the clubhouse.

Continue until you reach a cross-track, which should be at least vaguely familiar, as it was the first you encountered on this walk, albeit from the opposite direction. Turn R here, and continue through some trees and then past two, separate farm outbuildings. When eventually you reach a fork (the track now a proper road surface), bear L, staying high on your existing track/ road. When you shortly reach another choice of tracks, where the road becomes unsurfaced again, continue straight on (the R of two options), noting as you pass it, a Battle of Roundway Down information sign.

The route continues along the track a little further until on the L, a fenced path is reached. Views of the scarp edge are now beginning to dominate, and are the forerunner to a grand finale to this walk. Head along the fenced path until you reach a small gate on the R, leading onto the downs. Now follow the scarp edge as it arcs round in a superb U-shape, offering glorious views, both west and of the scarp's own individual spurs. Here one can truly be said to be at the far western extremity of the Pewsey Downs, and if you have also stood on Martinsell Hill in the far east, the poignancy of this spot will be all the more apparent.

Bear L and east-north-east with the downland crest eventually turning your back on the view west. Shortly after passing the last, solitary hilltop tree, you will spy another Battle of Roundway Down sign. Continue past it to a gate on your L, leading onto a fenced path. Soon you will reach a track, where you turn R, then L, then R again to continue. Stay on the track for some distance (heading south-south-east) noting that it becomes a road surface just before bearing to the L.

Follow the road, which now continues in an easterly direction, and when you reach and pass a wooded area turn L uphill, following the road for a few moments to return to your car.

Longer Itineraries

The very best of the Pewsey Downs

The more I walk over these lovely downs from a variety of approaches, the harder it becomes to construct a route that really does encapsulate their very best aspects in one manageable outing. Thus, what follows is a rather subjective attempt to provide two options (outlined only in brief), for those wishing to enjoy an extended exploration of this magnificent area.

To complete a circular walk, a section of the Kennet and Avon Canal is a must. However, it is important that it does not become predominant, otherwise the walk could no longer be said to be 'the best of the downs', however enjoyable it may be. With this thought in mind, I would suggest a starting point on the canal either in or near Wilcott, or at Honeystreet. This way, one can warm up along the towpath (heading west), before ascending the downs.

Probably the finest ascent onto the downs scarp is from All Cannings, where the twin summits of Clifford's Hill beckon, sending a delicious spur right down to the roadside, as if to say 'come and climb me'. Then Tan Hill and the roof of Wiltshire can be easily reached, with the Wansdyke providing a superb link between the county's two highest points (Tan Hill and Milk Hill).

Walker's Hill follows, and then the crest of the downs can be enjoyed and savoured all the way to Martinsell Hill, where the vast panorama never disappoints. (Note that on reaching Huish Hill, it is preferable to stay high, crossing the A345 where Walk 4 begins, rather than descending to Oare.) Curving round from Martinsell Hill, one can then enjoy more indescribable views from Giant's Grave, before dropping reluctantly off the downs, into Oare.

Lanes from Oare lead back to the canal to complete an unforgettable round if you started in Wilcott, or to any easy finish along the canal, beneath Woodborough Hill and Picked Hill, if you set out from Honeystreet.

Alternatively, if you don't mind an out-and-back route, there's arguably no finer way to enjoy the downs than by following their crest east to Martinsell Hill and then west in return, via Giant's Grave, Oare and a steep re-ascent of the downs from the foot of Huish Hill. If tempted, All Cannings is again probably the best place to begin, however, you could extend the walk still further, by starting out from Bishop's Cannings, further west; but be warned you will have to get a move on to complete the walk in one day.

The MWW: Wootton Rivers to Devizes

A new trans-Wiltshire trail was officially opened in April 2007 (extended in September of the same year), of 55 (now 68) miles duration. Stage two begins in Wootton Rivers and follows a glorious route over the downs, via Martinsell Hill, along the Wansdyke to Morgan's Hill, before turning south to traverse the eastern escarpment of Roundway Hill. Then a gentle descent into Devizes completes the stage. As a linear route, there is probably no better way to experience the best of the Pewsey Downs. For more information see page 77.

Across the Pewsey Downs - north to south

Another delightful opportunity presents itself to those wishing to cross the downs and return in the same day.

Should such a prospect appeal, I would suggest you begin in East Kennett, following Walk 10 to the Wansdyke, but then continuing south to Walker's Hill and down into Alton Barnes (now Walk 7 in reverse), to join the canal for the short stretch to All Cannings (lunch could be taken in either Honeystreet or All Cannings).

Then you should head north, back onto the downs via Clifford's Hill and the Tan Hill plateau to join, with consummate ease, Walk 11, striding out on Allington Down, before eventually descending back to East Kennett. This option probably represents the best way to experience the southern and northern periphery of the area.

Note that the north to south (as opposed to south to north)

option, is preferable because of the lunch possibilities on offer in Honeystreet and All Cannings, and due to the superb final section of the outing, atop Allington Down.

Wet Weather Alternatives - along the Kennet & Avon Canal

When the weather is inclement and heading up onto the downs seems impractical, the Kennett and Avon Canal can make an interesting alternative. East of Devizes and through the Vale of Pewsey the towpath is not a cycle way, and thus is pleasantly quiet. Stretches of the footpath can be very boggy after persistent, heavy rain, but views are often open and uninterrupted, the downs filling the skyline to the north.

Three out-and-back walks, with a village either end, present themselves. From west to east they are Bishops's Cannings to All Cannings return, All Cannings to Honeystreet return and Honeystreet to Wilcott return.

Should the weather improve significantly while you are on the towpath, you could quite easily change your plans and work in a stretch of the downs too.

Concluding Remarks

Dear reader, this region (albeit small) offers so much scope for walkers of every kind and type; children can climb their first big hill, the less agile wander along downland crests, casual strollers have their horizons extended, seasoned outdoor enthusiasts (jaded by many expeditions) find fresh excitement, nature lovers discover numerous points of interest and even upland fanatics enjoy the juxtaposition of easy walking, a pleasant climate and dramatic hill-top panoramas.

Blessed with the opportunity for walks of a circular nature, the possible permutations are almost endless, and go well beyond the confines of this book. The walks described, will arguably take you through the very best of this special region, but don't fail to explore further, from angles of your own; just take especial care to ensure you consider the sensitive needs of landowners as you do so.

Enjoy these quiet and peaceful downs, never taking them for granted but rather revelling in every opportunity they provide for peaceful, challenging and scenically diverse fulfilment.

Lapwing, a handsome bird of the open fields, ditinguished by its cry 'peewit' and its fine crest

Acknowledgements

I would like to thank the staff of the Rights of Way Department, Wiltshire County Council (Richard Broadhead – Manager – especially) for providing vital information about existing rights of way, open access and the DEFRA scheme. Heartfelt thanks also go to Ken Watts, one of Wiltshire's foremost historical, landscape experts, whose advice and friendship have been both invaluable and an inspiration. Special thanks also to my sister-in-law, Joan Alsop, who produced all of the sketch maps for this guidebook.

Finally, my deepest gratitude is reserved for Roger Jones, editor and publisher, whose kindness, skill and professionalism has resulted in a publication with which I am delighted, and which could never have been achieved alone.

Further Reading

Exploring Historic Wiltshire Vol 1 (Ken Watts, Ex Libris Press).

The Marlborough Downs (Watts Ken, Ex-Libris Press). If you want to read an eloquent, inspirational, well researched and authoritative commentary on the delights of the Marlborough Downs, especially where they encroach on the Vale of Pewsey (the area focussed on in the present book), then there is no finer account than this. Already the author of seven books on Wiltshire, Ken Watts is well placed to provide a unique insight, being an enthusiast and expert simultaneously.

The Vale of Pewsey (John Chandler, Ex-Libris Press). A scholarly examination of the Vale of Pewsey, from a highly respected historian.

Pubs and Inns Featured in the Guidebook

On a west to east basis, the pubs and inns mentioned in this guidebook are as follows:

The Crown Inn, Bishop's Cannings	01380 860218
The New Inn, Coate	01380 860644
The King's Arms, All Cannings	01380 860328
The Barge Inn, Honeystreet	01672 851705
The White Hart, Oare	01672 562273
The Royal Oak, Wootton Rivers	01672 810322

Also by James Alsop:

The official guidebook to the latest long distance trail through Wiltshire, that traces much of the county's finest downland, including the Pewsey Downs from east to west.

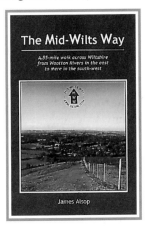

The Mid-Wilts Way has proved a hit since it was published in July 2007. In this handy guidebook, James Alsop describes the course of his 55-mile long waymarked trail across Wiltshire. The starting point is Wootton Rivers on the Kennet & Avon Canal in the east and the finish is the attractive viallge of Mere in the south-west. Sweeping views and quiet countryside predominate and even the villages possess a serenity unmatched in many other parts of southern Engalnd.
• The walk is described in six stages of similar length, and in an east to south-west direction
• Points of interest along the way are highlighted in the relevant section
• Sketch maps and illustrations complement the guide

Format uniform with the present book
and published by Ex Libris Press
80 pages; ISBN 978-1-903341-42-1; Price £5.95

About the Author

James Alsop has been a keen walker for many years, having climbed more than 130 separate Scottish mountains, several Welsh peaks and a selection of hills and mountains on the island of Mallorca. However, despite a previous obsession with upland areas, his walking interests are now far more holistic; West Wales, the Exmoor coast and the south west region generally being favoured walking areas. Most recently, Wiltshire – the county of his birth – has increasingly occupied first place in his outdoor affections.

James lectures in Tourism and Business at Wiltshire College. He is married to Kate, and they have two daughters, Evangeline and Isabella.

More books on Wiltshire from Ex Libris Press ~

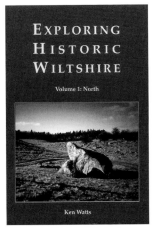

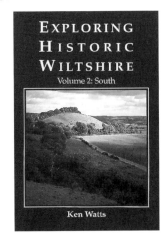

EXPLORING HISTORIC WILTSHIRE Volume 1: North
& EXPLORING HISTORIC WILTSHIRE Volume 2: South
by Ken Watts
Each book deals with six districts of the county describing their history, landscapes and artistic associations. In addition there are a number suggested walks.
Both books are fully illustrated with photographs & sketch maps and both are indexed.
Volume 1 – 176 pages; ISBN 0-948578-85-8; Price £7.95
Volume 2 – 176 pages; ISBN 0-948578-92-0; Price £7.95

THE MARLBBOROUGH DOWNS
by Ken Watts
Fully illustrated with photographs
& line drawings; Indexed
192 pages
ISBN 0-948578-15-9
Price £7.95

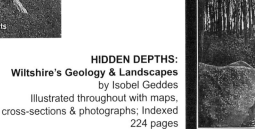

HIDDEN DEPTHS:
Wiltshire's Geology & Landscapes
by Isobel Geddes
Illustrated throughout with maps,
cross-sections & photographs; Indexed
224 pages
ISBN 1-903341-05-1
Price £9.95

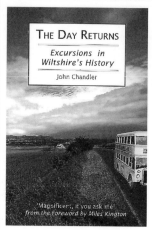